A Note From Rick Renner

I am on a personal quest to see a "revival of the Bible" so people can establish their lives on a firm foundation that will stand strong and endure the test as end-time storm winds begin to intensify.

In order to experience a revival of the Bible in your personal life, it is important to take time each day to read, receive, and apply its truths to your life. James tells us that if we will continue in the perfect law of liberty — refusing to be forgetful hearers, but determined to be doers — we will be blessed in our ways. As you watch or listen to the programs in this series and work through this corresponding study guide, I trust you will search the Scriptures and allow the Holy Spirit to help you hear something new from God's Word that applies specifically to your life. I encourage you to be a doer of the Word He reveals to you. Whatever the cost, I assure you — it will be worth it.

> Thy words were found, and I did eat them;
> and thy word was unto me the joy and rejoicing of mine heart:
> for I am called by thy name, O Lord God of hosts.
> — Jeremiah 15:16

Your brother and friend in Jesus Christ,

Rick Renner

Keeping Your Thinking Straight

Copyright © 2021 by Rick Renner
P.O. Box 702040
Tulsa, OK 74170

Published by Rick Renner Ministries
www.renner.org

ISBN 13: 978-1-68031-962-0

eBook ISBN 13: 978-1-68031-963-7

How To Use This Study Guide

This five-lesson study guide corresponds to *"Keeping Your Thinking Straight" With Rick Renner* (Renner TV). Each lesson in this study guide covers a topic that is addressed during the program series, with questions and references supplied to draw you deeper into your own private study of the Scriptures on this subject.

To derive the most benefit from this study guide, consider the following:

First, watch or listen to the program prior to working through the corresponding lesson in this guide. (Programs can also be viewed at **renner.org** by clicking on the Media/Archives links.)

Second, take the time to look up the scriptures included in each lesson. Prayerfully consider their application to your own life.

Third, use a journal or notebook to make note of your answers to each lesson's Study Questions and Practical Application challenges.

Fourth, invest specific time in prayer and in the Word of God to consult with the Holy Spirit. Write down the scriptures or insights He reveals to you.

Finally, take action! Whatever the Lord tells you to do according to His Word, do it.

For added insights on this subject, it is recommended that you obtain Rick Renner's books *How To Keep Your Head on Straight in a World Gone Crazy: Developing Discernment for These Last Days.* You may also select from Rick's other available resources by placing your order at **renner.org** or by calling 1-800-742-5593.

TOPIC

Getting Rid of Wrong Thinking

SCRIPTURES

1. **James 1:1** — James, a servant of God and of the Lord Jesus Christ, to the twelve tribes which are scattered abroad, greeting.
2. **James 1:13** — Let no man say when he is tempted, I am tempted of God: for God cannot be tempted with evil, neither tempteth he any man [with evil].
3. **James 1:17** — Every good gift and every perfect gift is from above, and cometh down from the Father of lights, with whom is no variableness, neither shadow of turning.
4. **James 1:18** — Of his own will begat he us with the word of truth, that we should be a kind of firstfruits of his creatures.
5. **James 1:19-21** — Wherefore, my beloved brethren, let every man be swift to hear, slow to speak, slow to wrath. For the wrath of man worketh not the righteousness of God: Wherefore lay apart all filthiness and superfluity of naughtiness, and receive with meekness the engrafted word, which is able to save your souls.

GREEK WORDS

1. "scattered abroad" — **διασπορά** (*diaspora*): the random scattering of seed; used to depict the scattering of Jewish believers
2. "will" — **βούλομαι** (*boulomai*): will, advise, counsel
3. "kind" — **τινα** (*tina*): certain, specific, notable
4. "firstfruits" — **ἀπαρχή** (*aparche*): new; the first; a new start; first fruits of a new kind of crop
5. "creatures" — **κτίσμα** (*ktisma*): newly created creatures; brand new creatures

6. "brethren" — ἀδελφός (*adelphos*): a term used to describe two or more who were born from the same womb; an endearing term used to describe those of one's own family; later used in a military sense to depict brothers in battle; a comrade; hence, brotherhood

7. "swift" — ταχύς (*tachus*): a runner who runs as fast as he can so he can reach the finish line before his competitors; this runner fiercely wants to win the race, so he puts everything else out of his mind, focuses on the finish line, and then presses forward to obtain the first-place prize; to move one's feet as fast as possible; to do something urgently; to do something as swiftly as possible

8. "hear" — ἀκούω (*akouo*): hear; comprehend, acoustics

9. "slow" — βραδύς (*bradus*): to be tardy, slow, delayed, late in time; handicapped

10. "speak" — λαλέω (*laleo*): speak, converse, communicate, talk

11. "wrath" — ὀργή (*orge*): silent resentment that suddenly gives way as an outburst of emotion; deeply felt anger suddenly released; a swelling, growing wrathful emotion that explodes in rage; wrath

12. "lay apart" — ἀποτίθημι (*apotithimi*): to lay something down; to lay something down and push it beyond reach so that it cannot be easily retrieved; a deliberate decision to make a permanent change of attitude and behavior; can be used to denote the removal of clothes

13. "filthiness" — ῥυπαρία (*rhuparia*): filthy; vile; soiled; dirty; obnoxiously filthy; especially used to denote filthy and smelly clothes

14. "superfluity" — περισσεία (*perisseia*): excessive; exceedingly; something so profuse that it can be likened to a river that is overflowing and flooding its banks

15. "naughtiness" — κακία (*kakia*): bad; evil; vile; foul

SYNOPSIS

The five lessons in this study on *Keeping Your Thinking Straight* will focus on the following topics:

- Getting Rid of Wrong Thinking
- 5 Steps To Change Your Thinking
- Keeping Your Thinking Straight About Religion
- Keeping Your Thinking Straight About Prejudice in the Church

• Keeping Your Thinking Straight About Economic Status and Money

The emphasis of this lesson:

James wrote to the persecuted believers who were scattered throughout the Roman Empire. In the midst of their troubles, they began to think God was allowing the devastation to enter their lives. He told them plainly that there is no evil in God and He doesn't bring evil into our lives. Right thinking about troubles and what God gives puts you in position to receive all the good, beneficial, profitable, and perfecting things He wants to give you.

How important is your thinking? It is *very* important. Your mind is the control center of your life. The Bible says, "For as he [a person] thinketh in his heart, so is he…" (Proverbs 23:7). The way you think and what you think about directly affect who you are. Every action you take and every word you speak is the result of the thoughts you think. Thus, the health of your mind is vital to the quality of your life.

Friend, we are living in the last of the last days, and just as Jesus and the prophet Paul forecasted, people are abandoning the timeless truth of Scripture and embracing unbelievable ideas and philosophies that are totally void of common sense. Now more than ever, it is crucial that we learn how to keep our thinking straight in a world that is going crazy.

James' Letter Was Written to
the Persecuted Believers Scattered Abroad

The believers in the First Century were experiencing great persecution, and the pressure had become so intense that their thinking was becoming distorted. In an effort to lovingly set them straight, James — the half-brother of Jesus and leader of the Church in Jerusalem — wrote them a powerful letter. He opened by saying, "James, a servant of God and of the Lord Jesus Christ, to the twelve tribes which are scattered abroad, greeting" (James 1:1).

The words "scattered abroad" identify specifically who James was writing to. This phrase is a translation of the Greek word *diaspora*, a very specific word that describes *the random scattering of seed*. When a farmer planted seed into his field, he could take his time and methodically plant one seed after another seed after another seed in a nice, neat row. Or he could reach his hand into a satchel of seed and grab a whole handful and begin throwing it randomly all over the field. That is exactly what the word *diaspora* depicts — and in this case it is a random scattering of *people*.

James used this word to denote what had happened to the believers as a result of the persecution they were suffering. History reveals that Christians were uprooted from their homes, their jobs, and their country and were dispersed like seed all over the eastern lands of the Roman Empire. In addition to losing their source of income and their place to live, they also lost their network of friends. Deeply discouraged, they began to wonder, *Is God allowing all these disastrous events to take place? Is all of this suffering somehow the will of God for us?*

In their distress, believers from all across the Roman Empire began writing letters to James asking him to explain what was going on. At that time, he was the most visible Jewish believer at the Church in Jerusalem. Needless to say, his mailbox became jam-packed with letters, and everyone seemed to be asking the same question: "Has God, for some reason and in some way, allowed all of this tragedy to come into our lives?"

Wrong Thinking About God Was Taking Them Down the Wrong Path

James answered their question in part by saying, "Let no man say when he is tempted, I am tempted of God: for God cannot be tempted with evil, neither tempteth he any man [with evil]" (James 1:13). Notice the first four words out of James' mouth: "Let no man say." In Greek, this is a very strong rebuke or prohibition that literally means, "I hear what you're saying, and I don't like it. Stop it and stop it now!" These believers weren't thinking right. They were saying when they were tempted that God was the One tempting them.

To this James said, "Let no man say when he is tempted, I am tempted of God…" (James 1:13). The word "tempted," which appears twice, is the Greek word *peiradzo*, and it means *to test, try, or tempt*. It describes Satan's repeated attempts to bring people down and destroy them. It is *a calculated test designed to cause one to fail, to falter, to stumble,* or *to bring destruction*. It is the very word used to describe the *temptation* Jesus experienced when He went without food for 40 days in the wilderness and the devil did everything he could to oust Jesus from His place of faith and His purpose.

Also notice the word "of." It is the Greek word *apo*, which means *away from* and denotes *something done from a distance* or *something done remotely*. The use of *apo* here implies these Christians believed God was doing something *remotely*. Although they didn't think God Himself was attacking them and bringing destruction into their lives, they were beginning to believe He was indirectly allowing it from a distance.

"God is God," they were saying. "And if He had wanted to stop these hardships, He could have stopped them. So since He didn't stop them, it must be His permissive will for us to go through them." This type of thinking is wrong, and that is why James essentially told them, "Let no man say when he is tempted that God is causing it. How dare you say that! How can you even think that God would do such a thing to you? That is just not the nature of God!"

There Is No Evil in God Nor Does He Bring Evil

To set their thinking straight, James declared, "…For God cannot be tempted with evil, neither tempteth he any man" (James 1:13). The phrase "God cannot be tempted" is the Greek word *apeirasmos*. The word *peirasmos* means *to be tried or to be tempted*. When the letter "a" is placed at the front of *peirasmos* to form *apeirasmos*, it signifies that *God cannot be tempted with evil*. Nothing in Him responds to evil, and He has no experience with evil.

The word "evil" is the Greek word *kakos*, and it describes *something evil, vile, foul, or destructive*. There is nothing evil, vile, or foul in God, and therefore, He cannot do anything evil, foul, or vile to anyone. He can't be tempted by evil, nor does He tempt people with it. When "evil" tried to come into Heaven in the person of Lucifer, God put a stop to it by casting Satan and those who rebelled with him out of His presence.

There is no evil in Heaven, and God doesn't bring evil into your life to test you. It is something He simply cannot do. If you think God permits evil to come into your life, you will remain in the evil trap of the enemy. However, if you think correctly and understand that the difficult situations you're facing are not sent from God, you will fight against them. Right thinking about trouble and trials is the first step to getting out of your trap.

Everything Good
Comes From God

James went on a few verses later to say, "Every good gift and every perfect gift is from above, and cometh down from the Father of lights, with whom is no variableness, neither shadow of turning" (James 1:17). Taking into account the original Greek text, this verse could be translated, "Anything *good, beneficial*, or *profitable* is from God, and He doesn't just give one gift; He keeps on giving and giving and giving. Everything He gives is *completing, maturing, and perfecting*." If we receive something from God, it *never takes away* — it *always adds to us*.

The Bible says these gifts "cometh down" from above. The phrase "cometh down" is the Greek word *katabaino*, which is a compound of the words *kata* and *baino*. The word *kata* describes *something that comes down so hard it is dominating or subjugating*, and the word *baino* means *to step down*. When the words *kata* and *baino* are compounded to form *katabaino*, it means *to be dominated or subjugated by something coming down very hard, like a downpour of rain*.

If you've ever been driving in a downpour, you know that rain can often come down so hard and heavy that you can't see anything in front of you. Sometimes the downpour is so dominating that you have to pull over to the side of the road and wait for the rain to stop. That is a picture of what the phrase "cometh down" means. God is so intent on blessing us that He is pouring down good and perfect gifts all around us.

Now, you may say, "If God is pouring good and perfect gifts on me, why am I not hit by one of those downpours occasionally?" The answer is simple — you must receive His gifts by faith. If your mind thinks and believes that God is causing or allowing your problems, you're not looking for or anticipating His goodness to pour into your life. If this is the way you've been seeing God, you have to work to renew your mind with the truth — that **every good gift and every perfect gift is from God above**.

Right thinking about what God gives puts you in position to receive all the good, beneficial, profitable, and perfecting things He wants to give you.

We Are a Brand-New Species

James continued his letter by saying, "Of his [God's] own will begat he us with the word of truth, that we should be a kind of firstfruits of his creatures" (James 1:18). The word "will" here is a translation of the Greek word *boulomai*, which describes *advice* or *counsel*. When you run into an issue you don't know how to deal with, you seek out sound advice — *boulomai* — from a counselor. In this verse, we see God seeking counsel from Himself. Of His own will, He chose to birth us by His truth — the Good News of Jesus Christ.

Jesus is the Word of truth! And we are born again by the incorruptible *good* Seed of Christ (*see* 1 Peter 1:23). James said this makes us "…a kind of firstfruits of his creatures" (James 1:18). The word "kind" in Greek is *tina*, and it describes *a certain, specific, notable kind*. Specifically, we are a notable "firstfruits" — from the Greek word *aparche*, meaning *new, the first*, or *a new kind of crop*. This brings us to the word "creatures," from the Greek word *ktisma*, which describes *newly created creatures* or *a brand-new species*.

That's God's desire for you and for the Church — that we be a people who do not know darkness, or anything connected to darkness. Instead, we are a people who live in the Light and experience the fruit of the Light.

James Placed Himself in the Trenches, Fighting Alongside His Brothers

When we come to James 1:19, we read, "Wherefore, my beloved brethren, let every man be swift to hear, slow to speak, slow to wrath." For a second time, James calls his readers "brethren," which is the Greek word *adelphos*, a term used to describe *two or more who were born from the same womb*. This endearing term was used to denote *those of one's own family* — including believers who were related spiritually, having been born out of the womb of God.

On a historical note, the word *adelphos* was later used in a military sense to depict *brothers in battle, a comrade*; or *a brotherhood*. It was first popularized by Alexander the Great, who was viewed as one of the greatest soldiers in human history. Every Greek soldier wanted to be affiliated with Alexander. So every now and then, he would host a huge award ceremony and call especially brave soldiers up on stage to stand with him. He'd wrap his arm around the soldier and say to all the adoring soldiers, "Let all of the empire know that Alexander is proud to be the brother (*adelphos*) of this soldier!" It was his way of saying, "Brother, you and I are in this fight together!" Hence, the word *adelphos* carried the idea of *camaraderie* and was the greatest honor that could be conferred upon a soldier.

By using the word "brother" (*adelphos*), James placed himself down in the trenches with the believers who were really struggling and blaming God for their problems. Instead of condemning them for struggling in their faith because of the persecution they were experiencing, he spoke words of praise that showed he was proud of them for staying in the fight and not giving up. At the same time, he was correcting the error in their thinking about God.

He Advised Them To Be *Swift To Listen*, *Slow To Speak*, and *Slow To Wrath*

With compassion yet firmness, James said, "…Let every man be swift to hear, slow to speak, slow to wrath" (James 1:19). In Greek, the word "swift" is *tachus*, which means *to move one's feet as fast as possible* or *to do something urgently* or *as swiftly as possible*. It pictures *a runner who runs as fast as he can so he can reach the finish line before his competitors*. This runner fiercely wants to win the race, so he puts everything else out of his mind, focuses on the finish line, and then presses forward to obtain the first-place prize.

James told his readers to be swift to "hear," which is the Greek word *akouo*, meaning *to hear* or *comprehend*. It is from where we get the word *acoustics*. What were they to hear and comprehend? That "Every good gift and every perfect gift is from above…" (James 1:17). When they were tempted to think that God had allowed tragedy to come into their lives, they were to shut their ears to it and run to the Word of God as fast as they could to renew their mind to this truth: "Every good gift and every perfect gift is from above…" They were to hear this and hear this and hear this until finally they comprehended it.

Along with being swift to hear, James also said to be "slow to speak." The word "slow" here is the Greek word *bradus*, which means *to be tardy, slow, delayed, or late in time*. It carries the idea of being *handicapped*. Essentially, James is saying, "When it comes to responding too quickly when you're overwhelmed by problems, it would benefit you to be a little handicapped in your speech." That's what the word "speak" — the Greek word *laleo* — in James 1:19 refers to. It means *to speak, converse, communicate, or talk*. Rather than say, "Oh, I guess God has allowed all of these troubles to come against me," James said, "Zip your lip! Slow down and be a little handicapped in your speech. Run to the truth."

James then adds, "…[Be] slow to wrath" (James 1:19). The word "slow" is again the Greek word *bradus*, meaning *to be tardy, slow, delayed, late in time,* or *handicapped*. And the word "wrath" in Greek is *orge*, which describes *silent resentment that suddenly gives way as an outburst of emotion*. This is *a deeply felt anger suddenly released — a swelling, growing wrathful emotion that explodes in rage*. Apparently, the believers James was writing to were carrying resentment toward God because they thought He had somehow remotely permitted all of the tragic events to pass into their lives. They were thinking wrong, which led to them talking wrong, and it was not producing anything good.

Recognize and Reject Wrong Thinking

James went on to say, "For the wrath of man worketh not the righteousness of God. Wherefore lay apart all filthiness and superfluity of naughtiness, and receive with meekness the engrafted word, which is able to save your souls" (James 1:20,21).

The words "lay apart" are a translation of the Greek word *apotithimi*, which is a compound of the words *apo* and *tithemi*. The word *apo* means *away* and in this verse carries the idea of *distance*. The word *tithemi* means *to place or to lay something down*. When these words are compounded to form *apotithimi*, it means *to lay something down and push it beyond reach so that it cannot be easily retrieved*. It denotes *a deliberate decision to make a permanent change of attitude and behavior*. *Apotithimi* is the same Greek word used to depict *the removal of old dirty clothes*.

When you come to the end of your day and it's time to go to sleep, what do you do to remove the clothes you've been wearing? Do you stand in front of the mirror and say, "Okay dirty clothes, I'm done with you. Come off my body this instant"? Of course not. To remove your dirty clothes, you must make a conscious decision and then use your hands and fingers to remove them from your body. You choose to unzip the zippers and push the buttons through the buttonholes and purposely remove what you have been wearing.

By using the word *apotithimi* — translated here as "lay apart" — James is telling us that when we hear the Word of God and we come to the realization that an area in our life doesn't line up with what the Word is saying, we have to make a decision to eliminate that wrong thinking from our lives. Simply recognizing something in us is not right will not bring change. We have to make a decision and take action. This is what it means to *repent* — to decide to turn away from sin, which includes wrong thinking, and choose to embrace and live in the truth.

It Is 'Filthiness and Superfluity of Naughtiness'

What are we to "lay apart"? James said "filthiness and superfluity of naughtiness" (James 1:21). The word "filthiness" is the Greek word *rhuparia*, and it describes *something obnoxiously filthy, vile, or soiled; something that is extremely base*. The word *rhuparia* is especially used to denote *filthy, smelly clothes*.

When we have a way of thinking, believing, or acting that is wrong and we allow it to continue in our lives unchecked, God's Word says it stinks with an unbearable stench. If we know that what we are thinking, believing, or doing is wrong and against God's Word, it is a grimy filthiness that we need to "lay apart" from our lives.

If filthiness goes unchecked in our lives, it leads to a "superfluity of naughtiness" (James 1:21). The word "superfluity" is the Greek term *perisseia*, and it describes *something excessive and so profuse that it can be likened to a swollen river that is overflowing and flooding beyond its banks*. James' use of this word tells us that if we don't get a grip on the wrong thinking in our lives, it will become worse and worse until it eventually overflows into every area of our lives — superfluity.

This brings us to the word "naughtiness," which is from the Greek word *kakia*, meaning *something bad, evil, foul, or rank*. It is putrid and has a dreadful stench. The word *kakia* is actually the word used in the gospels to describe people who were grievously vexed by demonic spirits.

Once a believer comes to the realization that his thinking, his actions, or his belief system is wrong, he has a choice: remain in it because it requires too much effort to change or do whatever is necessary to break free. Again, wrong thinking that is not dealt with will eventually become like a swollen river that is overflowing its banks and flooding every area of our life. That is not God's plan for you.

Instead of tolerating "filthiness and superfluity of naughtiness," God wants you to *lay it apart*. Specifically, He wants you to lay apart the wrong thinking that He's somehow bringing or allowing bad things to come into your life. God cannot be tempted by evil, nor does He tempt *us* with evil. He only brings good and perfect gifts into our life.

In our next lesson, we will explore five steps you can take to change your thinking.

STUDY QUESTIONS

Study to shew thyself approved unto God, a workman that needeth not to be ashamed, rightly dividing the word of truth.
— 2 Timothy 2:15

1. What new insights did you learn from this lesson about the book of James, the scattering of First-Century believers, and getting rid of wrong thinking?

2. What connection can you see between James 1:18 and Paul's words in Second Corinthians 5:17?

3. When James says to be "slow to speak," he is urging us not to respond too quickly when we're overwhelmed by problems — to be a little "handicapped" in our speech. What do these verses say to you about controlling the words of your mouth?

    *   Psalm 34:12-14 and 1 Peter 3:9-11

    *   Proverbs 13:3; 21:23

    *   Psalm 141:3 and John 14:30

PRACTICAL APPLICATION

But be ye doers of the word, and not hearers only, deceiving your own selves.
—James 1:22

1. When James talks about being "tempted," he's describing *a calculated test designed to cause one to fail, to falter, to stumble, or to bring destruction.* What are you going through right now that meets this description? Take a few moments to share what is weighing heavy on your mind.

2. If you're experiencing trials and troubles like the believers in the Early Church, you may have begun to wonder, *Is all of this suffering somehow the will of God for me? Is He allowing all these difficulties to come into my life from a distance?* Be honest. Are you carrying resentment toward God? What are you learning from this lesson to shatter that lie and set your thinking straight?

3. God used James to speak encouragement and correction to the persecuted believers in the First Century who were not thinking straight about Him. Who has God used to bring correction and speak encouragement into your life?

TOPIC

5 Steps To Change Your Thinking

SCRIPTURES

1. **James 1:21** — Wherefore lay apart all filthiness and superfluity of naughtiness, and receive with meekness the engrafted word, which is able to save your souls.

2. **James 1:22-25** — But be ye doers of the word, and not hearers only, deceiving your own selves. For if any be a hearer of the word, and not a doer, he is like unto a man beholding his natural face in a glass: For he beholdeth himself, and goeth his way, and straightway forgetteth what manner of man he was. But whoso looketh into the perfect law of liberty, and continueth therein, he being not a forgetful hearer, but a doer of the work, this man shall be blessed in his deed.

GREEK WORDS

1. "lay apart" — **ἀποτίθημι** (*apotithimi*): to lay something down; to lay something down and push it beyond reach so that it cannot be easily retrieved; a deliberate decision to make a permanent change of attitude and behavior; can be used to denote the removal of clothes

2. "filthiness" — **ῥυπαρία** (*rhuparia*): filthy; vile; soiled; dirty; obnoxiously filthy; especially used to denote filthy and smelly clothes

3. "superfluity" — **περισσεία** (*perisseia*): excessive; exceedingly; something so profuse that it can be likened to a river that is overflowing and flooding its banks

4. "naughtiness" — **κακία** (*kakia*): bad; evil; vile; foul

5. "receive" — **δέχομαι** (*dechomai*): to take quickly, to take readily, or to take with a receptive and welcoming attitude

6. "meekness" — **πραΰτης** (*prautes*): a strong-willed person who has learned to submit his will to a higher authority

7. "engrafted" — **ἔμφυτος** (*emphutos*): engrafted; subsequently implanted

8. "able" — **δύναμαι** (*dunamai*): has power, has ability

9. "save" — **σῴζω** (*sodzo*): salvation; wholeness in every part of life in an eternal or temporal sense; salvation that brings delivering and healing power that results in wholeness; can be translated to heal

10. "souls" — **ψυχή** (*psuche*): mind, will, and emotions

11. "But be ye doers" — **ποιητής** (*poietes*): to do; to do creatively; to perform; the root for the word poet

12. "hearers only" — **ἀκροατής** (*akroates*): used to describe individuals who audited a class rather than take it for credit; hence, it depicted a hearer only, or one who had no intention of applying what he heard; he merely attended the class but had no plans to implement what was taught

13. "deceiving your own selves" — **παραλογίζομαι** (*paralogidzomai*): a miscalculation; a wrong analysis of facts or of a situation

14. "beholding" — **κατανοέω** (*katanoeo*): to think down; to consider; to deeply contemplate

15. "natural face" — **πρόσωπον τῆς γενέσεως αὐτοῦ** (*prosopon tes geneseos autou*): the face of his birth; the face he was born with

16. "glass" — **ἔσοπτρον** (*esoptron*): highly polished metal; a mirror

17. "beholdeth" — **κατανοέω** (*katanoeo*): to think down; to think thoroughly; to consider; to deeply contemplate

18. "goeth" — **ἀπέρχομαι** (*aperchomai*): to be on one's way

19. "forgetteth" — **ἐπιλανθάνομαι** (*epilanthanomai*): to turn away from and forget; to deliberately ignore, to disregard, or to completely forget

20. "looketh into" — **παρακύπτω** (*parakupto*): from **παρά** (*para*) and **κύπτω** (*kupto*); the word **παρά** (*para*) means alongside and **κύπτω** (*kupto*) means to stoop or to lower oneself; to stoop lower to take a

closer look; to deeply investigate; to peer deeply into a mirror to gain a truthful and realistic view of what the mirror shows

21. "liberty" — ἐλευθερία (*eleutheria*): liberty, freedom; freedom from slavery

22. "continueth therein" — παραμένω (*parameno*): from παρά (*para*) and μένω (*meno*); παρά (*para*) means alongside, and μένω (*meno*) means to stay in one spot or to abide; to remain next to, to remain alongside of; to persevere

23. "blessed" — μακάριος (*makarios*): ridiculously blessed; blessed with God's blessings; to be envied; blessed beyond measure

24. "deed" — ποιέω (*poieo*): to do; to do creatively; to perform; the root for the word poet

SYNOPSIS

Wrong thinking that is not dealt with will lead to devastation and destruction in our lives. The fact is, all of us have areas in our lives right now where we are not seeing things clearly, and until we realize just how stinking our thinking is, we're going to stay stuck in the mire and muck. God has given us His Word to serve as a truth detector in our lives — to reveal where we're in error and show us the right way to live. It is His Word that renews our mind and saves our soul from the contaminated thinking of our fallen flesh and this sinful world.

The emphasis of this lesson:

Changing your thinking involves an ongoing commitment and decision to submit to God's authority, eliminate any opposing influences, and receive His Word into your life. To receive God's Word with meekness is to say no to your own opinions, views, and ways, and open your heart to hear and obey His truth. When you find creative ways to do what God says — despite the inconvenience — you become a doer of the Word.

How Do We Get Rid of Wrong Thinking?

At the end of Lesson 1, we began examining God's instructions in James 1:21, where James wrote, "Wherefore lay apart all filthiness and superfluity of naughtiness, and receive with meekness the engrafted word, which is able to save your souls." Let's review the meaning of the key words in this verse in order to get this truth deep down inside of us.

"Lay apart" is the Greek word *apotithimi*. It is the compound of two words — *apo* and *tithemi*. The word *apo* means *away*, and the word *tithemi* means *to place or to put down*. When these words are joined to form *apotithimi*, it means *to lay something down and push it beyond reach so that it cannot be easily retrieved.* It is *a deliberate decision to make a permanent change of attitude and behavior.* This word *apotithimi* is the very word used by the Greeks to denote *the removal of dirty clothes at the end of the day.*

To get rid of the clothes you've been wearing all day and put on fresh garments, you must make a decision to take them off. You then intentionally use your hands and fingers to remove the "old" clothes from your body. In the same way, in order to get rid of wrong thinking, we have to come to the realization that an area in our life doesn't line up with the Word, and then we have to decide to "take off" or remove what is wrong. Simply recognizing that something in us is not right will not magically bring change. We have to make a decision and take action.

"Filthiness and [the] superfluity of naughtiness" is what James called the old, dirty clothing that we need to remove. In Greek, the word "filthiness" is *rhuparia*, and it describes *something filthy, vile, soiled, dirty, or obnoxiously filthy.* This word was especially used to denote *filthy and smelly clothes.* When we have a way of thinking, believing, or acting that is wrong — and we allow it to continue in our lives unchecked — God's Word says it stinks with an unbearable stench.

When filthiness begins to grow out of control, James said it becomes "superfluity of naughtiness." The word "superfluity" is the Greek word *perisseia*, which describes *something excessive, exceeding, or so profuse that it can be likened to a river that is overflowing and flooding its banks.* James used this word to warn us that if we don't get a grip on what is wrong in our lives, it will become worse and worse until it eventually flows into every area of our lives and even affects others.

The word "naughtiness" is from the Greek word *kakia*, and it describes *something bad, evil, vile, or foul.* It was the very word used in the gospels to describe individuals who were "vexed" with demon spirits. "Naughtiness" (*kakia*) is something putrid and has a dreadful stench and must be dealt with.

We must make a choice. Once we come to the realization that our thoughts, words, or actions are wrong, we can choose to remain in that situation because it requires too much effort to change, or we can do whatever is necessary to break free. Instead of tolerating "filthiness and superfluity of naughtiness" in our lives, we are to obey God's instruction and take them off, lay them down, and push them so far away that we cannot reach them to pick them up again.

Receive God's Word With Meekness

Once we lay apart all filthiness and superfluity of naughtiness, James said, "...Receive with meekness the engrafted word, which is able to save your souls" (James 1:21). First, notice the word "receive." It is the Greek word *dechomai*, and it means *to take quickly*, *to take readily*, or *to take with a receptive and welcoming attitude*. God wants us to readily and quickly welcome His Word into our hearts and mind with *meekness*.

Very often when people hear the word *meek*, they think it means *weak*, but that is not the case. The word "meekness" here is the Greek word *prautes*, and it describes *a strong-willed person who thinks he is right but has learned to submit his will to a higher authority*. That is, he has chosen to deliberately set aside his opinion and deny what he thinks and how he feels about things in order to submit to and trust in what someone else is saying.

For example, let's say you were taught or grew up believing that God sends or allows tragedy and trouble into your life, and then you hear a teaching like this from James 1:17, which says, "Every good gift and every perfect gift is from above...." The only way this word of truth is going to take root inside you is if you say, "I know what I have believed and what my experience has been in the past. But I'm going to choose — by the grace of God — to lay all of that thinking aside and push it out of my reach. I'm going to submit to and believe God's Word, which says, "...God cannot be tempted with evil, neither tempteth he any man. Every good gift and every perfect gift is from above..." (James 1:13,17). Making yourself think and submit to God's thoughts (His Word) is really what the word *meekness* means.

The Word Becomes 'Engrafted' in You

What are we to receive with meekness? James said, "...the engrafted word, which is able to save your souls" (James 1:21). The word "engrafted" here is the Greek word *emphutos*, and it signifies *something that is planted in you at a later time in life*. It is *something with which you were not born*.

The best illustration of the word "engrafted" is an *organ transplant*. Anyone in need of a new organ is in a pretty serious situation. In fact, if you need one, the doctors may say you will likely die if you don't get one. When you receive a donated organ, it is not originally yours; it is from another source and is placed in you.

Interestingly, immediately after receiving the new organ, the body attempts to reject it. Innately it knows that the organ is not original to the body and begins treating it as a foreign object. The only way the body will accept the new organ is if the recipient takes medication for the remainder of his life. All of this imagery is packed into the word "engrafted" (*emphutos*).

Think about it. When the truth of God's Word comes to you, it's not something you were born with — it comes to you later in life. Your flesh — which is your old, un-renewed human nature — immediately recognizes the Word as a foreign intruder and begins to war against it. All that you have experienced and been taught in life that is contrary to the Truth rises up to reject it. The only way God's Word will take root in you and save your soul is if you receive it with "meekness" (*prautes*). That is, you have to say no to your own opinions, views, and ways, and open your heart to hear and obey the Word.

5 Steps To Eliminate Wrong Thinking and Receive the Engrafted Word

1. **Submission** – You have to be submitted to the authority of God. You have to choose to come under His authority, believe what He says in His Word, and then do it, regardless of what you think or how you feel.

2. **Elimination** – You must then eliminate your own opinions and feelings and anything else that would distract or keep you from submitting to God's authority. Take them off — lay them apart — and determine not to reach out and pick back up thoughts that would keep you from submitting and aligning yourself with God.

3. **Decision** – Decide that you will not veer from what God says, but that you will instead remain committed to the principles of His Word.

4. **Continuation** – Your decision is not a one-time event, but an ongoing commitment to continually eliminate wrong thinking, and remain in submission to the Word of God.

5. **Reception** - As you walk out the first four steps, you will finally begin to receive the Word of God into your life, which "is able to save your souls."

God's Word Has Saving Power!

Scripture says the engrafted Word of God "…is able to save your souls" (James 1:21). The word "able" in Greek is *dunamai*, which means *it has power and ability*. What does the Word of God have power to do? James said it "…is able to save your souls." The word "save" is the Greek word *sodzo*, and it describes *salvation* or *wholeness in every part of life in an eternal or temporal sense*. The Word brings *salvation that releases delivering and healing power that results in wholeness*. That is what the power of God's Word will do in your *soul*.

The Greek word for "souls" is *psuche*, and it describes *a person's mind, will, and emotions*, which is what New Testament writers clearly understood to be components of *the soul* or *inner life*. The soul is where our problems are. That's where we need the greatest transformation. The moment we're saved and make Jesus our Lord and Savior, our spirit is transformed and filled with the Holy Spirit. Our soul, on the other hand, is transformed throughout our lifetime. This is what the Bible calls *sanctification*.

As you continue to receive the Word of God with meekness again and again and again, it has the divine power to save your soul, which means it brings *salvation* or *wholeness* to your mind, your emotions, and your will. The Word will change the way you think, how you feel, and how you make decisions.

Be a 'Doer,' Not Just a 'Hearer'

James goes on to tell us, "But be ye doers of the word, and not hearers only, deceiving your own selves" (James 1:22). In the Greek, "be ye doers" essentially means *be ye becoming*. In other words, *start where you are — start today* — and begin obeying what the Word says. God doesn't expect immediate change; He just wants you to get started.

The word "doer" is from the Greek word *poieo*, and it means *to creatively do something*. It is where we get the word "poet." A poet has a creative flare for expressing thoughts and ideas. By using the word *poieo*, the Bible is saying, "Don't wait until it is convenient or easy to obey the Word. Find a way to creatively do what God says to do." Remember, you are a "disciple"

— a *committed learner* of Christ who is listening to, learning, and applying His teachings.

Scripture urges us to be *doers* of the Word and "not hearers only." The phrase "hearers only" is the Greek word *akroates*, a term that was used to describe *individuals who audited a class rather than take it for credit.* Hence, a "hearer only" is *one who had no intention of applying what he heard.* This person merely attended the class but had no plans to implement what was taught.

What Kind of Christian Are You?

James 1:22 tells us that there are *two* kinds of Christians: The first is a *doer*, or one who hears the Word of God and does whatever he can to creatively obey what it says. The second is a *hearer only* —one who shows up and is physically present to hear the Word, but mentally and spiritually he or she is disengaged. That is, this person has no intention of ever doing what the Word says.

The Bible goes on to say that anyone who is merely "auditing church" and has no plans on putting anything they hear into practice is "deceiving themselves." The word "deceiving" is the Greek word *paralogidzomai*, which essentially means *to make a miscalculation.* It is a librarian term that depicts a scholar placing documents side-by-side to compare and analyze the information, but he comes to the wrong conclusion.

Basically, James is saying, "If you think things are going to improve and be great just because you *hear* the Word, you have made a tragic miscalculation — your analysis is wrong." Yes, you need to hear the Word, but you also have to find a way to creatively put it into practice. It is in the *doing* of the Word that it really takes root and begins to operate in you and save your soul.

How Are You Responding to What You See in the Mirror?

James continued in the next verse saying, "For if any be a hearer of the word, and not a doer, he is like unto a man beholding his natural face in a glass" (James 1:23). The word "beholding" is the Greek word *katanoeo*, which means *to think down, to consider,* or *to deeply contemplate.* What is he pondering? Scripture says his "natural face," which in Greek literally means *the face of his birth* or *the face he was born with.* The word "glass" is the Greek word *esoptron*, which is the term for *highly polished metal* that served as a *small hand mirror* that could only be used to look at one small area at a time.

When most people get up in the morning and look in the mirror at the face they were born with, they see things about themselves they don't like — things they need to change. Their hair is a mess, their teeth need brushing, there are bags under their eyes, and the list goes on. How one responds to what he sees in the mirror is the key to whether or not positive change is experienced.

In the same way, God's Word serves as a hand mirror to show us what we look like spiritually and what we need to change. Thankfully, the Holy Spirit doesn't show us everything that needs to change in our lives all at once. Instead, He deals with us one area at a time. For instance, He shows us one area of thinking that is wrong and then gives us the *power* and *desire* to change it (*see* Philippians 2:12,13). He then moves the mirror and shows us another area of thinking that is wrong. Again, how we respond to what we see in the mirror determines whether or not we experience positive change.

One Who Only Hears the Word
Ignores the Holy Spirit and Does Nothing

The Bible goes on to say that the person who is a hearer only, "…Beholdeth himself, and goeth his way, and straightway forgetteth what manner of man he was" (James 1:24). The word "beholdeth" is again the Greek word *katanoeo*, which means *to think down*, *to think thoroughly*, *to consider*, or *to deeply contemplate*. Although the hearer only sees what needs to be changed, he doesn't deal with it. Instead, he "goeth his way," which in Greek means *he is on the move and quickly on his way.*

After seeing what needs to be fixed, Scripture says he "…forgetteth what manner of man he was" (James 1:24). The word "forgetteth" in Greek is *epilanthanomai*, and it means *to turn away from and forget*; *to deliberately ignore*, *to disregard*, or *to completely forget.* Sadly, there are many Christians living like this. God speaks to them and shows them things about themselves in the Word that need to be addressed, but they do nothing about it.

Those who are "hearers only" of the Word view change as too difficult. After seeing what needs to be adjusted in their lives, they begin to delude themselves into thinking things are not as bad as they appear. Although they hear the Word, they don't stay in the Holy Spirit's presence long enough to allow Him to do the work only He can do and let His truth really sink in and penetrate their heart.

The Doer Obeys the Word and Blessings Follow

Great things happen when a "doer" looks into the Word! James 1:25 says, "But whoso looketh into the perfect law of liberty, and continueth therein, he being not a forgetful hearer, but a doer of the work, this man shall be blessed in his deed." The illustration of the mirror continues, only now the mirror changes from a hand-held size to a much larger, table-sized mirror.

The phrase "looketh into" is a translation of the Greek word *parakupto*, which is a compound of the words *para* and *kupto*. The word *para* means *alongside*, and *kupto* means *to stoop* or *to lower oneself*. When these words come together to form *parakupto*, it means *to stoop lower to take a closer look* or *to deeply investigate*. It is the picture of *one peering deeply into a mirror to take a close-up, truthful, and realistic view of what the mirror shows so that he or she can make a correction.*

The believer who is serious about changing the way he thinks and acts continues to hover over the Word until he understands what needs to be changed and allows the Spirit to do the work that only He can do. That's what the Bible means when it says "continueth therein." This phrase is the Greek word *parameno*, taken from the words *para* and *meno*. The word *para* means *alongside*, and *meno* means *to stay in one spot or to abide*. When these words are compounded, it means *to remain next to, to remain alongside of*, or *to persevere*.

The doer of the Word keeps looking and keeps looking and keeps looking into "the perfect law of liberty" — not a law of bondage, but a freedom-producing law. The word "liberty" is the Greek word *eleutheria*, which describes *liberty* or *freedom*, and it signifies *a slave that has been emancipated from slavery*. This word tells us that if we will look deeply into the Word of God, receive it with meekness, and do what it says, it will set us free from every type of slavery and bondage in our lives.

James went on to say that the doer of the Word, "...shall be blessed in his deed" (James 1:25). The word "blessed" here is the Greek word *makarios*, which means *ridiculously blessed* or *supremely blessed with God's blessings*. This person is so blessed beyond measure, they are to be envied! In particular, the Bible says they will be supremely blessed in their "deed" — the Greek word *poieo*, which again means *to do creatively* or *to perform*. It is the root for the word *poet*.

The "doer" continues to hover over and observe the Word until he sees what is wrong in his life made right. He sees the truth and says to himself, *I will live by this Word and obey it fully. And if I'm wrong in any area of my life, I will do whatever I need to do to adapt myself and get into agreement with the Word.* It is the "doer" of the Word that is ridiculously and supremely blessed.

In our next lesson, we will learn what the Bible has to say about pure religion — what it is and what it isn't.

STUDY QUESTIONS

Study to shew thyself approved unto God, a workman that needeth not to be ashamed, rightly dividing the word of truth.
— 2 Timothy 2:15

1. The Bible says if you *continue* in God's Word, you will be supremely "blessed" (*see* James 1:25). Continuing in the Word is the key. Read Second Timothy 3:14-17, Second Corinthians 3:12-18, and Jesus' words in John 8:31 and 32. In your own words, describe the connection between *continuing* in the Word and *experiencing transformation*. (Also *consider* Joshua 1:8 and Psalm 1:1-6.)

2. Have you ever heard something from Scripture and struggled to believe you could do it? You're not alone. Thankfully, God has given us some encouraging promises to refute this lie of the enemy. Consider what He says in Deuteronomy 30:11-14 and Philippians 4:13. What's the Holy Spirit showing you in these passages? (Also consider Matthew 19:26; Mark 9:23, and Luke 1:37.)

PRACTICAL APPLICATION

**But be ye doers of the word, and not hearers only,
deceiving your own selves.
—James 1:22**

1. Being a "doer" of the Word means not waiting until it's convenient or easy to obey what it says. It is finding creative ways to obey and do what God said. Be honest. Would you say you're more of a "doer" of the Word or a "hearer only"? What would those closest to you say? What would God say about you?

2. In what areas of your life do you tend to be more of a "hearer only"? Are these areas the Holy Spirit has been bringing to your attention? Pause and pray, *Lord, why am I struggling to obey You in these areas? Please forgive me and strengthen me to do what You're directing me to do. In Jesus' name.*" Now be still and listen. What is the Holy Spirit showing you?

3. James 1:21 urges us to "…Receive with meekness the engrafted word, which is able to save your souls." Receiving the "engrafted" Word is like experiencing an organ transplant you can't live without. How does this analogy magnify the vital importance of feeding on God's Word? Pray and ask the Holy Spirit, *What can I eliminate from my daily routine to make room for more time in God's Word? Please show me and help me understand and put into practice what You teach me. In Jesus' name. Amen.*

LESSON 3

TOPIC
Keeping Your Thinking Straight About Religion

SCRIPTURES

1. **James 1:26,27** — If any man among you seem to be religious, and bridleth not his tongue, but deceiveth his own heart, this man's religion is vain. Pure religion and undefiled before God and the Father is

this, To visit the fatherless and widows in their affliction, and to keep himself unspotted from the world.

1. **James 2:1** — My brethren, have not the faith of our Lord Jesus Christ, the Lord of glory, with respect of persons.

GREEK WORDS

1. "seem" — δοκέω (*dokeo*): to estimate; to have an opinion; to judge
2. "religious" — θρῆσκος (*threskos*): one outwardly observant of religious actions and duties
3. "bridleth" — χαλιναγωγέω (*chalinagogeo*): to constrain by a bridle; to hold in check by a bridle
4. "deceiveth" — ἀπατάω (*apatao*): to deceive; to cheat; to lead into error; to seduce; to give a distorted impression
5. "his own heart" — καρδίαν αὐτοῦ (*kardian autou*): the heart of himself; his own heart; where we derive the word cardiac
6. "religion" — θρῆσκος (*threskos*): one outwardly observant of religious actions and duties
7. "vain" — μάταιος (*mataios*): vain; waste; empty; futile; hollow; aimless; purposeless; useless; senseless
8. "pure religion" — θρησκεία καθαρὰ (*threskeia kithara*): from θρῆσκος (*threskos*) and καθαρός (*katharos*); the word θρῆσκος (*threskos*) one outwardly observant of religious actions and duties; the word καθαρός (*katharos*) means cleansed, pure, free of undesirable toxins or unclean elements; compounded, religion that is cleansed, pure, free of undesirable toxins or any form of uncleanness; clean religion
9. "undefiled" — ἀμίαντος (*amiantos*): unpolluted, unspotted, unstained, free from contamination
10. "before God" — παρὰ τῷ Θεῷ (*para to Theo*): alongside of God; near to God
11. "the Father" — πατήρ (*pater*): a loving father with all the caring attributes of fatherhood
12. "to visit" — ἐπισκέπτομαι (*episkeptomai*): to look upon, to physically visit, or to provide help for those in need, and it was even used to denote the provision of medical care
13. "fatherless" — ὀρφανός (*orphanos*): from this term that we derive the word orphan; in New Testament times, it described not only children left without a parent, but also included the idea of abandonment

14. "widows" — χήρα (*chera*): uniquely describes widows in the traditional sense of the word; used by Jesus in Matthew 23:14 and Luke 4:26 to describe women who were bereft of their spouses due to death

15. "affliction" — θλῖψις (*thlipsis*): great pressure; crushing pressure; to suffocate; the brunt of society; a horribly tight, life-threatening squeeze; a situation so difficult it caused one to feel stressed, squeezed, pressured, or crushed

SYNOPSIS

When it comes to keeping our thinking straight, another area we need to know about and understand is that of *religion*. Is there such a thing as good, pure religion? If so, what does it look like and what does the Bible have to say on the subject? As with other practical areas of Christian living, James weighs in on this topic and offers a number of eye-opening insights to empower and equip us to honor God and be a blessing to others.

The emphasis of this lesson:

Many people have different ideas of what it means to be religious, but only God's view really matters. Pure religion that is untainted and free of contamination is to visit and care for the fatherless and widows in their affliction and to keep ourselves unspotted from the world. The thing that is most near and dear to God's heart is caring for people in need.

Outward Appearances
Can Sometimes Be Deceiving

Immediately after James taught on the importance of being a doer of the Word, he turned his attention to the subject of religion, and said:

> **If any man among you seem to be religious, and bridleth not his tongue, but deceiveth his own heart, this man's religion is vain. Pure religion and undefiled before God and the Father is this, To visit the fatherless and widows in their affliction, and to keep himself unspotted from the world.**
> **—James 1:26,27**

These two verses are simply bursting with wisdom, so let's back up and begin to unpack what the Holy Spirit is saying through James, starting in verse 26. He says, "If any man among you seem to be religious, and bridleth not his tongue, but deceiveth his own heart, this man's religion is vain." The word "seem" here is the Greek word *dokeo*, which means *to estimate* or *to have an opinion*. In context here, the word "seem" indicates *a self-assessment* or *judging on oneself*.

The fact is many people have ideas and preconceived notions as what it means to be "religious," but none of our opinions matter. Only God's view is important. The word "religious" in Greek is *threskos*, and it describes *one outwardly observant of religious actions and duties*. On the outside, it appears this person is exemplary in every way, but the words coming out of his mouth are the real litmus test of their character.

Self-Deception is a Dangerous Condition of One's Own Heart

James said if he "bridleth not his tongue," something is not right. In Greek, the word "bridleth" is *chalinagogeo*, and it means *to constrain by a bridle* or *to hold in check by a bridle*. It is the very word used to describe the bridle placed on a horse in order to lead and guide it in the direction desired. Thus, James is telling us that if a person seems to be and claims to be religious, but he is unable to control his tongue, he "...deceiveth his own heart..." (James 1:26).

The word "deceiveth" is the Greek word *apatao*, which means *to deceive, to cheat*, or *to lead into error*. It can also mean *to seduce* or *to give a distorted impression*. In this case, this individual has seduced himself and ended up with an inaccurate, twisted view of who he or she really is. Honestly, it doesn't matter how loud we sing in worship, how many times we go to church, how many candles we light, or how many hours we pray. If we don't have control over the words coming out of our mouth, we've deceived our own heart into thinking we're something that we're not.

The phrase "his own heart" in Greek is *kardian autou*, and it means *the heart of himself* or *his own heart*. The word *kardian* is from where we derive the words *cardiac* and *cardiac arrest*. It is the word for the *heart*. This verse lets us know that deception is a heart issue. If we focus on our outward activities and good deeds but fail to look at what's in our heart and what's coming out of our mouth, we've deceived ourselves, and our "religion is vain."

Once more we see the word "religion" — the Greek word *threskos*, describing *one outwardly observant of religious actions and duties*. And the word "vain" in Greek is *mataios*, which depicts *something vain, empty, futile, or hollow*. It carries the idea of being *aimless; purposeless; useless; or senseless*. It is this type of *vain* demonstration that causes unsaved people in the world to say that all Christians are hypocrites. When we say one thing and then do the opposite, we give Jesus a bad name.

Probably one of the greatest examples of this hypocrisy is hearing someone who claims to be a loving Christian going around gossiping about others. Although this person may attend church regularly, give their tithe faithfully, and serve dutifully in several areas of ministry, the fact that they're constantly cutting people down and talking about their faults and flaws invalidates their witness. This is a vivid picture of a person whose religion is in vain.

A Picture of 'Pure Religion'

To help us truly grasp this vital truth, James goes on to say, "Pure religion and undefiled before God and the Father is this, To visit the fatherless and widows in their affliction, and to keep himself unspotted from the world" (James 1:27). If we really want to touch the heart of God and capture His attention, we would be wise to understand this passage and put it into practice.

The phrase "pure religion" is a translation of the Greek words *threskeia kithara*, which is derived from the words *threskos* and *katharos*. The word *threskos* describes *one outwardly observant of religious actions and duties*; and the word *katharos* means *cleansed, pure, free of undesirable toxins or unclean elements*. When these words are joined to form *threskeia kithara*, it describes *religion that is cleansed, pure, free of undesirable toxins or any form of uncleanness*. Taken as one phrase, this new word literally means *clean religion*.

The fact that the Bible says there is "pure religion" tells us that there is also *impure* religion. The dirty, unclean version is what gives all of us — even those demonstrating pure religion — a bad name. James said that pure religion is "undefiled before God." This word "undefiled" is the Greek word *amiantos*, which describes *something unpolluted, unspotted, unstained, and free from contamination.*

The phrase "before God" in Greek is *para to Theo.* The word *para* we have seen several times, and it means *alongside.* The phrase *to Theo* means *of God.* Hence, "before God" indicates being *alongside of God* or *near to God* and carries the idea of being *near to the heart of God.*

This brings us to the phrase "the Father" — the Greek word *pater*, which describes *a loving father with all the caring attributes of fatherhood.* He loves his children and cares for those who are in need. In this passage, James pulls back the curtain to reveal the religious activity — the outward acts of service — that are really near and dear to the heart of God. They are: "... To visit the fatherless and widows in their affliction, and to keep himself unspotted from the world" (James 1:27).

'Visit the Fatherless'

The words "to visit" are a translation of the Greek word *episkeptomai*, which is from the word *epi*, meaning *over*, and the word *skopos*, which means *to look* and is from where we get the words *telescope* and *microscope.* When *epi* and *skopos* are compounded to form *episkeptomai*, it means *to look upon, to physically visit*, or *to provide help for those in need.* Interestingly, this word was even used to denote *the provision of medical care* to those who could not pay for it themselves.

It is not enough to see someone in need from a distance and just wave at them and throw up a prayer to Heaven. Yes, prayer is important — but so is taking action to help meet people's needs. Caring for the needy — providing food, clothing, and shelter to those who don't have it — touches the heart of God deeply! Although the people who need the help cannot pay us back, God can — and He will!

It is important to note that James specifically mentions visiting the "fatherless." In Greek, this is the word *orphanos*, which is where we derive the word *orphan.* Although in some cases the parents are still living, the children have been abandoned and left to themselves with no parental care or guidance. In certain parts of the world like Russia, these kids are often called *social orphans*; they are living with their parents but have basically been abandoned by them. They aren't providing their children with things like clothes to wear, food to eat, or a place to live. They lack guidance, and, for all intents and purposes, they are fatherless and motherless.

In New Testament times, the word *orphanos* described not only *children left without a parent*, but also included *those that had been abandoned* — including adults. When you and I know that someone is suffering abandonment — by their family, by a spouse, or by their friends — and they're living in isolation feeling so alone, we have a God-given responsibility to visit them, inspect their needs, and see what we can do to help them in their situation.

'Visit the Widows in Their Affliction'

Not only are we to minister to the needs of the fatherless but also "…visit the widows in their affliction…" (James 1:27). The word "widows" here is the Greek word *chera*, which uniquely describes *widows in the traditional sense of the word*. It is the very word used by Jesus in Matthew 23:14 and Luke 4:26 to describe *women who were bereft of their spouses due to death*.

When a woman becomes a widow, she enters a very challenging season. Financial pressures often arise. What she did for years — in many cases decades — with the accompaniment of her spouse is now totally different. Things her husband may have handled — such as paying the bills, taking care of the yard and car, and maintaining the repairs on the house — are now solely her responsibilities. Likewise, she often feels socially out of place. The dynamics of many of her relationships are very different as her husband is no longer in the picture.

This perspective helps us see why James said to visit widows in their "affliction." The word "affliction" is the Greek word *thlipsis*, which describes *great pressure* or *crushing pressure*. It refers to *a horribly tight, life-threatening squeeze; a situation so difficult it causes one to feel stressed, squeezed, pressured, or crushed*. Many widows face pressuring hardships such as help with housing and food, medical needs, or other physical needs that leave a person struggling to get up and face each day.

According to James 1:27, God has given believers the responsibility to reach out and help widowed women who are struggling as a result of losing a spouse. It is good, clean, and acceptable religion before God for us to visit and assist widows in these circumstances.

It's true that we live in a day and age when insurance companies pay death benefits, the government offers assistance to women who've lost their spouses, and many widows are not suffering financially. However, there are still many widowed women who suffer great financial and social need when their spouses die, and God commands us to do whatever we can to be a blessing to them in their times of suffering.

What Else Does James Say To Be Aware of?

When we come to the second chapter of James, he shifts his focus to another important subject, and it concerns avoiding prejudice within the Church. Specifically, James said, "My brethren, have not the faith of our Lord Jesus Christ, the Lord of glory, with respect of persons" (James 2:1).

The phrase "with respect of persons" in Greek refers to *judging others by their outward appearance.* This includes judging someone's skin color, their clothing, their ethnic background or nationality, their economic status, their education or lack thereof, or anything else pertaining to their outward appearance.

What does the Holy Spirit tell us through James to help us keep our thinking straight regarding prejudice in the Church? That will be our focus in Lesson 4.

STUDY QUESTIONS

**Study to shew thyself approved unto God, a workman that needeth not to be ashamed, rightly dividing the word of truth.
— 2 Timothy 2:15**

1. As believers, when we "talk the talk" but don't "walk the walk," we give Jesus a bad name. What did God say to David would happen because of his sinful actions (*see* 2 Samuel 12:14)? How does this passage, along with Paul's words in Romans 2:21-24, put the fear of God in you?

2. One of the most damaging sins that is often overlooked in the Church is *gossip.* What does the Bible have to say about unrestrained lips? Check out God's perspective in Proverbs 11:13; 17:9; 18:6-8; 20:19; 26:20 and Leviticus 19:16.

3. Pure religion is inseparably linked with *God's love.* According to First John 3:16-18, how is real love — as well as pure religion — demonstrated? (Also consider Isaiah 58:6-11.)

PRACTICAL APPLICATION

But be ye doers of the word, and not hearers only,
deceiving your own selves.
— James 1:22

1. According to Scripture, there are many children who have parents but are still considered "fatherless" because they have been abandoned and left to themselves with no parental care or guidance. What children do you know that fall into this category? In what practical ways can you fulfill God's wishes to "visit" and care for them?

2. How about *widows*? Do you know any women whose husbands are no longer alive that may be experiencing all the challenges of doing life alone? Who are they, and how might you lend a helping hand to these individuals?

LESSON 4

TOPIC

Keeping Your Thinking Straight About Prejudice in the Church

SCRIPTURES

1. **1 Samuel 16:6,7** — And it came to pass, when they were come, that he looked on Eliab, and said, Surely the Lord's anointed is before him. But the Lord said unto Samuel, Look not on his countenance, or on the height of his stature; because I have refused him: for the Lord seeth not as man seeth; for man looketh on the outward appearance, but the Lord looketh on the heart.

2. **James 2:1-4** — My brethren, have not the faith of our Lord Jesus Christ, the Lord of glory, with respect of persons. For if there come unto your assembly a man with a gold ring, in goodly apparel, and there come in also a poor man in vile raiment; And ye have respect to him that weareth the gay clothing, and say unto him, Sit thou here in a good place; and say to the poor, Stand thou there, or sit here under

my footstool: Are ye not then partial in yourselves, and are become judges of evil thoughts?

3. **Colossians 3:11** — Where there is neither Greek nor Jew, circumcision nor uncircumcision, Barbarian, Scythian, bond nor free: but Christ is all, and in all.

4. **Galatians 3:28** — There is neither Jew nor Greek, there is neither bond nor free, there is neither male nor female: for ye are all one in Christ Jesus.

5. **Revelation 5:9** — And they sung a new song, saying, Thou art worthy to take the book, and to open the seals thereof: for thou wast slain, and hast redeemed us to God by thy blood out of every kindred, and tongue, and people, and nation.

GREEK WORDS

1. "respect of persons" — **προσωπολημψία** (*prosopolepsia*): looking at one's face or looking at their external appearance; describes acceptance based on one's face or being affected by external appearance

2. "have" — **ἔχω** (*echo*): have, hold, or possess

3. "Lord Jesus Christ" — **Κυρίου ἡμῶν Ἰησοῦ Χριστοῦ** (*Kuriou hemon Iesou Christou*): as a phrase, The Supreme Lord, Jehovah, Yahweh Who Saves, The Anointed One, the Messiah

4. "assembly" — **συναγωγή** (*sunagoge*): meeting place; congregation

5. "[of] yours" — **ὑμῶν** (*humon*): of yours, making it very personal

6. "gold ring" — **χρυσοδακτύλιος** (*chrusodaktulios*): from **χρυσός** (*chrusos*) and **δακτύλιος** (*daktulios*); the word **χρυσός** (*chrusos*) pictures the highest grade of gold and the most expensive form of gold; the word **δακτύλιος** (*daktulios*) is a fabulous ring that is highly decorated

7. "goodly apparel" — **ἐσθῆτι λαμπρᾷ** (*estheti lampra*): from **ἐσθής** (*esthes*) and **λαμπρός** (*lampros*); the word **ἐσθής** (*esthes*) pictures a robe or vestment; the word **λαμπρός** (*lampros*) means bright, gorgeous, magnificent, resplendent, shining, sumptuous; as a phrase, gorgeous or sumptuous clothing; obviously expensive and belonging to someone with financial means

8. "poor man" — **πτωχός** (*ptochos*): meaning one who crouches or cowers like a beggar; beggarly; poor; deeply destitute; lacking in earthly resources; a pauper

9. "vile raiment" — **ῥυπαρός ἐσθῆτι** (*rhuparos estheti*): from **ῥυπαρός** (*rhuparos*) and **ἐσθής** (*esthes*); the word **ῥυπαρός** (*rhuparos*) means filthy dirty, grimy, or rank; the word **ἐσθής** (*esthes*) pictures a robe or vestment; as a phrase, filthy dirty, grimy, rank clothes; pictures one who dresses as if he lives in squalor

10. "respect" — **ἐπιβλέπω** (*epiblepo*): to look upon; to fix your gaze upon; to regard with favor

11. "gay clothing" — **ἐσθῆτα τὴν λαμπρὰν** (*estheta ten lampran*): means bright, gorgeous, magnificent, resplendent, shining, sumptuous; as a phrase, gorgeous or sumptuous clothing; obviously expensive and belonging to someone with financial means

12. "Sit thou here" — **Σὺ κάθου ὧδε καλῶς** (*Su kathou hode kalos*): You be seated here in a place of honor and respect

13. "poor" — **πτωχός** (*ptochos*): from a word meaning one who crouches or cowers like a beggar; beggarly; poor; deeply destitute; lacking in earthly resources; a pauper

14. "Stand thou there" — **Σὺ στῆθι ἐκεῖ** (*Su stethi ekei*): You, stand over there, in a place that is out of the way, less visible, and less honorable; get out of the way; stand over there

15. "judges" — **κριτής** (*krites*): critics; opinionated; one who passes judgment

16. "evil" — **πονηρός** (*poneros*): malicious or malignant; foul, vile, hostile, and vicious; it includes not only that which is dangerous to the physical body but also to that which is dangerous to the spirit or mind; an act or attitude that is wicked, unholy, and impure

17. "thoughts" — **διαλογισμός** (*dialogismos*): reasonings; deliberations; inward reasonings or judgments; inward reasoning that is self-based and confused

SYNOPSIS

In our first lesson, we focused on why it is so important to recognize and reject wrong thinking — especially the erroneous idea that God brings evil into our lives. In Lesson 2, we learned five steps to change our thinking along with the indescribable value of receiving the "engrafted" Word of God, which has the power to save our souls. Then in Lesson 3, we examined what "pure, undefiled religion" is in the eyes of God and how our words and actions reveal the true quality of our devotion to Him.

In this lesson, we will turn our attention to another area that James addresses where we need to keep our thinking straight, and that is in how we deal with prejudice in the Church.

The emphasis of this lesson:

Essentially, prejudice is pre-judging others based on their external appearance. No one is born with it. Rather, it is imparted to us by others and often develops as a result of difficult life experiences. Although there are many different types of prejudice, God disproves them all. He doesn't judge anyone based on external factors, and neither should we.

God Corrected the Prophet Samuel for being Prejudice

It is sad to say but more times than not, we tend to judge others based solely on their outward appearance, and that is just not right. Even Samuel, the highly respected and anointed prophet of God made this same mistake when he was searching for the man who would replace Saul as king of Israel. After the Lord had prompted Samuel to go to the house of Jesse in Bethlehem to anoint one of his sons to be the next king, the Bible says:

> **And it came to pass, when they were come, that he looked on Eliab, and said, Surely the Lord's anointed is before him. But the Lord said unto Samuel, Look not on his countenance, or on the height of his stature; because I have refused him: for the Lord seeth not as man seeth; for man looketh on the outward appearance, but the Lord looketh on the heart.**
> **— 1 Samuel 16:6,7**

Eliab — which we understand was Jesse's oldest son — appeared to be the obvious choice to be the next king. But God quickly corrected Samuel and gave us all a powerful life-principle to live by: Although man looks at the outward appearance, God looks at the heart. This is how He wants us to begin to look at others. Rather than judge people by what we see on the surface, He wants us to be led by His Spirit and see people for who they really are inside.

Prejudice Abounds...
Even in the Church

James addressed the issue of prejudice in the Church early on in his letter by saying, "My brethren, have not the faith of our Lord Jesus Christ, the Lord of glory, with respect of persons" (James 2:1). In this verse, the phrase "respect of persons" is a translation of the Greek word *prosopolepsia*, which literally means *looking at one's face* or *looking at their external appearance*. It describes *acceptance based on one's face* or *being affected by external appearance*.

What are some of the most common ways that people are judged by external appearance?

The most widespread form of prejudice is based on skin color. It seems that most people with a darker skin color often feel prejudice against them. But that is not the only issue. Many people live their lives having prejudice toward *specific people groups* like...

- Native Americans
- Asians
- Jews
- Germans (especially after WWII)
- Mexicans
- Chinese
- Japanese (especially during and after WWII)

It is interesting to note that people not only have prejudice toward those with a different skin color or eye shape, but also against people with the *same* skin color. For example, people can have a predominantly "white"-colored skin and still feel prejudice toward one another. In other words, just because people all have the same skin color doesn't mean they get along well.

If you go to certain places in Europe (where everyone is generally "white-skinned"), there are certain French people who are prejudice toward the British, and vice-versa. Likewise, there are Germans who don't like Italians and Italians that don't like Germans. Add to that, there are many surrounding Europeans who don't like Polish people. And on and on it goes.

Other Types of Prejudice

There is also **age prejudice** where those who are old are viewed as useless because of their physical limitations. Then there are others who view young people as not viable because they have little money, are inexperienced, and tend to be selfish.

There is also **class prejudice** where the rich take sides against the poor and the poor unite against the rich. Interestingly, there is even prejudice between rich people and between poor people. Class prejudice also involves education: those who are educated sometimes are biased against those who are uneducated.

Some people have **disability prejudice** where they believe those who are handicapped can't contribute anything to life, which is not true at all. Stephen Hawking, who was wheelchair bound and couldn't speak clearly, was a genius and made a great impact on modern science.

There are some who have **orphan prejudice**. This is a mindset that believes orphans cannot be trusted because they are all street kids who are thieves. Similarly, there is **homeless-person prejudice** in which all homeless people are seen as irresponsible failures that are likely dealing with drug and alcohol addiction. Although some live up to this stereotype, it is not always the case.

How about the age-old battle of the sexes — male vs. female? We would call this **sex prejudice**. Then there's what we might label **unmarried prejudice** where people believe something is wrong with a person, and that's why he or she isn't married. There is even **family prejudice** where people with few or no children have a disdainful attitude toward families with large numbers of kids.

You may have seen or experienced **weight prejudice**. This is when individuals who are thin/skinny judge those who are overweight. In some cases, those who are overweight will have a negative opinion about those who are skinny, believing them to be feeble and unable to take life seriously.

Then there is **foreigner prejudice** where local workers hold a grudge against foreigners for intruding into "their" territory and taking "their" jobs. This is somewhat related to **city prejudice** in which citizens of one town will have a strong rivalry against a close neighbor (i.e. Moscow/St. Petersburg).

Accent prejudice is also a source of division. For instance, those with a Yankee accent are often viewed by southerners as snobbish, and those from the south are viewed by northerners as stupid.

Clothing prejudice also exists. This occurs when people immediately make a negative judgment against someone based on the clothes they're wearing. Sometimes those who dress more formal (elegant dress/coat and tie) are viewed as stuffy and out-of-touch, whereas those who wear jeans and more casual clothes are sometimes viewed as disingenuous, shallow, or immature.

Of course, **religious prejudice** has been around since the beginning of creation. Today, there is prejudice between denominations and within denominations. It is even common to see a biased rivalry between larger churches and smaller churches — or between churches of the same size.

How Does a Person Become Prejudice?

The fact is prejudice comes in all shapes and sizes, and it knows no boundaries. No one is born with prejudice — it is not natural or innate. New-born babies feel no prejudice against anyone. On the contrary, prejudice is imparted to us by others. More specific, it is imparted by culture and society as well as family and friends. Many times prejudice develops as a result of difficult life experiences.

Regardless of where it came from, prejudice in all forms is wrong. As one person plainly put it, prejudice is not a *skin* issue — it's a *sin* issue. God doesn't judge people based on superficial, external factors, and neither should we. Writing under the inspiration of the Holy Spirit, the apostle Paul said:

> **There is neither Jew nor Greek, there is neither bond nor free, there is neither male nor female: for ye are all one in Christ Jesus (Galatians 3:28).**

> **Where there is neither Greek nor Jew, circumcision nor uncircumcision, Barbarian, Scythian, bond nor free: but Christ is all, and in all (Colossians 3:11).**

These verses tell us plainly that we need to keep our thinking straight when it comes to prejudice and not tolerate any form of it in our lives and in the Church.

James Called Jesus
'Lord Jesus Christ'

Returning to the second chapter of James, he writes, "My brethren, have not the faith of our Lord Jesus Christ, the Lord of glory, with respect of persons" (James 2:1). Once more, James addresses his readers as "brethren" — the Greek word *adelphos*. There is no judgment or prejudice in his voice. Instead, he places himself on their level and calls them his *comrades* — fellow fighters in the faith, born from the same womb of God.

When James says, "…Have not the faith of our Lord Jesus Christ," the word "have" is the Greek word *echo*, which means *to have, to hold*, or *to possess*. In the context here, he is saying, "Don't have… Don't hold… Don't possess the faith of our Lord Jesus Christ…." Interestingly, this is only the second time this designation — "Lord Jesus Christ" — appeared in written text. Remember, James is the oldest book of the New Testament. Hence, the title "Lord Jesus Christ" had never been formally written prior to this epistle.

Here for a second time, straight from the mouth of Jesus' stepbrother, we hear James say, "…Have not the faith of our Lord Jesus Christ…" (James 2:1). The word "Lord" is from the Greek word *kurios*, which means *supreme lord*. It is the very word translated as *Jehovah* in the Old Testament Septuagint, which James would have used and referred to when he wrote his letter.

The word "Jesus" means *Yahweh saves*. It is a declaration that *He is Yahweh* and *He is a Savior*. And the word "Christ" is the Greek term *Christos*, which means *The Anointed One, the Messiah*. When we put this whole phrase together — *Kuriou hemon Iesou Christou* — it means, *The Supreme Lord, Jehovah, Yahweh Who Saves, The Anointed One, the Messiah*. That's who Jesus is, and that's what we're saying every time we call Him "Lord Jesus Christ."

As we mentioned earlier, the phrase "respect of persons" in James 2:1 is a translation of the Greek word *prosopolepsia*, which literally means *looking at one's face* or *looking at their external appearance*. In context here, James is saying, "Do not judge others or base your acceptance of them on their face or external appearance."

Financial Prejudice on Display

In the very next verse, James began providing us a specific example of what prejudice looks like, saying, "For if there come unto your assembly a man with a gold ring, in goodly apparel, and there come in also a poor man in vile raiment" (James 2:2). In this instance, two men entered the church: a rich man and a poor man.

First notice the word "assembly." It is the Greek word *sunagoge*, which is where we get the word *synagogue*. It describes *a meeting place* or *a congregation*. James qualified what meeting place it was by using the word "[of] yours" — the Greek word *humon* — which zeros in on them and made it very personal.

What was the rich man wearing? James said he had a "gold ring." The Greek word for "gold" is *chrusos*, and it pictures *the highest grade of gold* and *the most expensive form of gold*. The word "ring" in Greek is *daktulios*, and it describes *a fabulous ring that is highly decorated*. The rich man was also wearing "goodly apparel," which in Greek is *estheti lampra* — from the words *esthes* and *lampros*. The word *esthes* pictures *a robe or vestment*; and the word *lampros* signifies *something bright, gorgeous, magnificent, resplendent, shining*, or *sumptuous*. As a phrase, "goodly apparel" (*estheti lampra*) depicts *gorgeous or sumptuous clothing* that is obviously expensive and belonging to someone with financial means.

The second man to enter the assembly was a "poor man." The word "poor" is a translation of the Greek word *ptochos*, meaning *one who crouches or cowers like a beggar* — probably out of embarrassment for the way he looks. This person is *beggarly, poor*, and *deeply destitute, lacking in earthly resources*. The word *ptochos* is the very word for a *pauper*.

James specifically said he was dressed in "vile raiment," which in Greek is *rhuparos estheti*, taken from the words *rhuparos* and *esthes*. The word *rhuparos* describes *something filthy dirty, grimy, or rank*; and the word *esthes* pictures *a robe or vestment*. As a phrase, *rhuparos estheti* ("vile raiment") describes *filthy dirty, grimy, rank clothes*. It is a picture of *one who dresses as if he lives in squalor*, and this is who was now entering the church meeting.

What Does Prejudice in the Church Look Like?

Here is a picture in James 2:3: "And ye have respect to him that weareth the gay clothing, and say unto him, Sit thou here in a good place; and say to the poor, Stand thou there, or sit here under my footstool." The word "respect" in this verse is the Greek word *epiblepo*. It is a compound of the word *epi*, meaning *upon*, and the word *blepo*, meaning *to gaze*. When these words come together to form *epiblepo*, it means *to look upon*; *to fix your gaze upon*; or *to regard with favor*.

Who were the believers fixing their gaze on and regarding with favor? It was the rich man dressed in "gay clothing." This is a translation of the Greek phrase *estheta ten lampran*, which means *bright, gorgeous, magnificent, resplendent, shining, or sumptuous*. As a phrase, it depicts *gorgeous or sumptuous clothing* that was obviously expensive and belonging to someone with financial means.

To this rich, affluent individual, the believers turned and said, "Sit thou here," which in Greek means, "You be seated here in a place of honor and respect." But to the "poor man" (*ptochos*) — the *pauper who crouches or cowers like a beggar and is deeply destitute and lacking in earthly resources* — the church leaders said, "Stand thou there," which in Greek literally means, "You, stand over there, in a place that is out of the way, less visible, and less honorable." It was the equivalent of saying, "Get out of the way and stand over there."

James Brought Firm Correction

At this point in his letter, James lowered the boom and brought correction to the believers, saying, "Are ye not then partial in yourselves, and are become judges of evil thoughts?" (James 2:4). The word "judges" here is the Greek word *krites*, which is the word for *critics*. Essentially, James questioned these believers, and asked them, "Have you not become *opinionated critics* who are passing judgment on others?"

He then called them out by saying they had "evil thoughts." In Greek, the word "evil" is *poneros*, which denotes *something malicious or malignant*. It is *foul, vile, hostile, and vicious*. It includes not only that which is dangerous to the physical body, but also that which is dangerous to the spirit or mind. This is *an act or attitude that is wicked, unholy, and impure*.

This brings us to the word "thoughts," which in Greek is the word *dialogismos* and refers to *inward reasonings* or *inward judgments that are self-based and confused*. Specifically, these believers were deliberating with themselves in their minds and falsely concluding by the poor man's outward appearance that he was vile and foul.

4 THINGS TO DO IF YOU HAVE PREJUDICE

If after reading through this lesson you discover that you have acted in prejudice, here is what you can do to make things right.

1. Become aware of your prejudices and ask the Holy Spirit to help you change. Find out what your prejudices are and ask the Holy Spirit to show you the source of your feelings.

2. Once you acknowledge your prejudice, acknowledge to God that you are wrong and repent. Ask the Holy Spirit to help you change the way you look at other people.

3. Spend less time with prejudiced people or prejudiced media. We are influenced by and tend to think like the people with whom we spend time. So be careful who you hang around. Likewise, be alert and aware of how the media affects you. It can make you think wrongly of a certain group of people.

4. Broaden your horizons and get some new experiences. Pray and ask the Holy Spirit to help you to reach out to someone in the group that you're tempted to be prejudiced against. Learn to work with them with an open mind and keep an open heart — trying to see what the world looks like through *their* eyes.

Keep in mind that when we get to Heaven, none of us is going to be judged by our skin color, nationality, financial worth, or any other superficial factor. The Bible says Jesus has "…redeemed us to God by [His] blood out of every kindred, and tongue, and people, and nation" (Revelation 5:9). With God's help, we can learn to keep our thinking straight about prejudice and begin to experience *now* the blessings of unity that Jesus prayed for us to enjoy (*see* John 17:11,21-23).

STUDY QUESTIONS

Study to shew thyself approved unto God, a workman that needeth not to be ashamed, rightly dividing the word of truth.
— 2 Timothy 2:15

1. Isaiah wrote a great deal about the coming Messiah, Jesus Christ — including what he said in Isaiah 11. What did he prophesy Jesus would do to avoid the trap of prejudice in verses 3-5? According to verse Isaiah 11:2, what was Jesus filled with that gave Him such discernment and the ability to not discriminate? (*See also* John 3:34.)

2. Did you know that the same empowerment Jesus had is available to you? Consider His promise in Luke 11:9-13, as well as Paul's words in Ephesians 5:18; 6:18; and Jude 20.

3. As you read through all the different forms of prejudice, which one (or ones) have people held against you? Are there any of which you have repeatedly been a victim? If so, which one and how has the experience affected you?

4. Be honest. Which forms of prejudice have you struggled with in the past? Are there any you are struggling with right now?

PRACTICAL APPLICATION

> But be ye doers of the word, and not hearers only,
> deceiving your own selves.
> — James 1:22

More than likely, after reading through this lesson you have come to the realization that you have acted in prejudice in the past — or you are dealing with a form of prejudice right now. Don't feel condemned. Simply receive the conviction of the Holy Spirit and repent for any wrong attitude. Then take some time to sit quietly and walk through the **"4 Things To Do If You Have Prejudice."** Answer each question honestly and make every effort to do the suggested activities — including lessening or eliminating prejudice in the entertainment you are consuming and spending time with someone in the group that you're tempted to be prejudiced against.

LESSON 5

TOPIC

Keeping Your Thinking Straight About Economic Status and Money

SCRIPTURES

1. **James 2:5-8** — Hearken, my beloved brethren, Hath not God chosen the poor of this world rich in faith, and heirs of the kingdom which

he hath promised to them that love him? But ye have despised the poor. Do not rich men oppress you, and draw you before the judgment seats? Do not they blaspheme that worthy name by the which ye are called? If ye fulfil the royal law according to the scripture, Thou shalt love thy neighbour as thyself, ye do well.

GREEK WORDS

1. "hearken" — Ἀκούσατε (*akousate*): hear; comprehend; where we get the word acoustics

2. "brethren" — ἀδελφός (*adelphos*): a term used to describe two or more who were born from the same womb; an endearing term used to describe those of one's own family; later used in a military sense to depict brothers in battle; a comrade; hence, brotherhood

3. "chosen" — ἐκλέγομαι (*eklegomai*): to call out, to select, to elect, or to choose; refers to individuals who were selected for a specific purpose; it conveys the idea of the privilege and honor of being chosen; it is so connected to the idea of privilege that those being selected should look upon themselves as honored, esteemed, and respected

4. "poor" — πτωχός (*ptochos*): meaning one who crouches or cowers like a beggar; beggarly; poor; deeply destitute; lacking earthly resources; a pauper

5. "world" — κόσμος (*kosmos*): the world; denotes systems in society

6. [to be]"rich" — πλούσιος (*plousios*): wealth so great it cannot be tabulated; vast wealth; extreme riches; incredible abundance; used by Plato to say no one was richer than legendary King Midas

7. "in faith" — ἐν πίστει (*en pistei*): describes a force that is moving forward

8. "heirs" — κληρονόμος (*kleronomos*): someone who inherits; inheritance, title-deed, legacy, heritable estate; in Christ, the lot has been cast in our favor and we are co-heirs with Christ

9. "kingdom" — βασιλεία (*basileia*): a realm of rule

10. "promised" — ἐπαγγέλλομαι (*epangellomai*): promise, guarantee, or pledge

11. "despised" — ἀτιμάζω (*atimadzo*): dishonor; insult; shameful

12. "draw" — ἑλκύω (*helkuo*): drag, lure, draw, as into a snare

13. "before" — εἰς (*eis*): into, right into

14. "judgment seats" — **κριτήριον** (*criterion*): place of arbitration; a place where judgment is given; the courts

15. "blaspheme" — **βλασφημέω** (*blasphemeo*): to slander; to accuse; to speak against; to speak derogatory words for the purpose of injuring or harming one's reputation; it also signifies profane, foul, unclean language; can refer to blaspheming the divine, but in general is any derogatory speech intended to defame, injure, or harm another's reputation; broader meaning includes nasty, shameful, ugly speech, or behavior intended to humiliate someone

16. "worthy" — **καλός** (*kalos*): good, noble, or superior; exceptional; of the highest quality; outstanding

17. "name" — **ὄνομα** (*onoma*): name or reputation

18. "ye are called" — **ἐπικαλέω ἐφ' ὑμᾶς** (*epikaleo eph' humas*): a name conferred upon you, referring to the name of Christ

19. "fulfill" — **τελέω** (*teleo*): to bring to fulfillment; to bring to maturity; to complete

20. "love" — **αγαπάω** (*agape*): the love of God; high-level love

21. "neighbor" — **πλησίον** (*plesion*): the one nearby you; any person near you in some way; neighbor

22. "well" — **καλός** (*kalos*): noble; good; superior behavior; exceptional

SYNOPSIS

In our last lesson, we learned about how the believers James was writing to had become confused in their thinking with regards to how they should treat the rich and the poor people who were coming to their churches. To address their error, James said:

> **My brethren, have not the faith of our Lord Jesus Christ, the Lord of glory, with respect of persons. For if there come unto your assembly a man with a gold ring, in goodly apparel, and there come in also a poor man in vile raiment; And ye have respect to him that weareth the gay clothing, and say unto him, Sit thou here in a good place; and say to the poor, Stand thou there, or sit here under my footstool: Are ye not then partial in yourselves, and are become judges of evil thoughts?**
> **—James 2:1-4**

According to this passage, it seems these Jewish believers were showing favoritism toward the wealthy and well-dressed and were treating the poor with contempt. As they offered the best seats in the church to the rich, the poor were being made to stand up or sit in the shadows out of sight. James lovingly but firmly rebuked their prejudice.

The emphasis of this lesson:

God has purposely chosen the poor of this world to be rich in faith. We are coheirs with Jesus Christ, and our faith in Him and His promises is moving us forward into the incredible inheritance and destiny we share with Him. Regardless of our socioeconomic status, when we are born again, everything begins to change. Because God doesn't show favoritism, we're all equal in His kingdom, and it's important to Him that we follow suit and treat others with the same unconditional love He's given to us.

James Lovingly, But Firmly
Addressed His Comrades in the Faith

Continuing to address the issue of economic status and money, James said, "Hearken, my beloved brethren, Hath not God chosen the poor of this world rich in faith, and heirs of the kingdom which he hath promised to them that love him? But ye have despised the poor. Do not rich men oppress you, and draw you before the judgment seats? Do not they blaspheme that worthy name by the which ye are called? If ye fulfil the royal law according to the scripture, Thou shalt love thy neighbour as thyself, ye do well" (James 2:5-8).

Look back at verse 5 and notice how James begins addressing his readers with the words, "Hearken, my beloved brethren…." The word "hearken" is the Greek word *akousate*, a form of the word *akouo*, from where we get the word *acoustics*. It means *to hear* or *to comprehend*. The use of this word was the equivalent of James saying, "Hear my words and really understand what I'm saying, my brethren."

Here, for a third time, James calls his readers "brethren," which is the Greek word *adelphos*, a term used to describe *two or more who were born from the same womb*. This term was not only endearing and used to describe those of one's own family, but it was also later used in a military sense to depict *brothers* — or *comrades* — in battle; hence, *a brotherhood*. It was James' way of placing himself on the same level as those he was writing to.

As Believers, We Are 'Chosen!'

Speaking rhetorically, James said, "…Hath not God chosen the poor of this world rich in faith…" (James 2:5). The word "chosen" here is extremely important. It is the Greek word *eklegomai*, which is a compound of the word *ek*, which is from where we get the word *exit*, and the word *lego*, which means *I say*. When these words are compounded to form *eklegomai*, it means *to call out, to select, to elect*, or *to choose*. What this tells us is if you are a Christian and belong to Christ, it's no accident.

Furthermore, the word *eklegomai* refers to *individuals who were selected for a specific purpose*. This means God has specifically selected you to do something extraordinary! This word also conveys the idea of *the privilege and honor of being chosen*. In fact, it is so connected to the idea of *privilege* that those being selected should look upon themselves as *honored, esteemed*, and *respected*.

Friend, we are chosen! God called us out of darkness into His marvelous light, and it doesn't matter what our economic status is today or how much money we have or lack of it. If we're chosen by God, we are *honored, esteemed*, and *respected* by Him. That said, every called-out, born-again child of God should be treated with honor, esteem, and respect.

The 'Poor' Have a Special Place in God's Family

James 2:5 says, "…God [has] chosen the poor of this world…." The word "poor" here is again the Greek word *ptochos* — the same word we saw in verses 2 and 3. It describes *one who crouches or cowers like a beggar because he is embarrassed about his condition*. This person is *beggarly, poor, deeply destitute*, and *lacking earthly resources*. *Ptochos* is the very word for a *pauper*.

Scripture says that God has personally selected the poor and deeply destitute of this "world." The word "world" here is not the word *geise*, which describes *the physical planet*. Rather, it is the Greek word *kosmos*, which denotes *all the systems of the world in society*.

Out of all the people in society, God has chosen those who are *paupers* in comparison to the rest of the world. A careful study of the First Century — the time in which the Church was birthed — reveals that the majority of those being born again were not high-level, blue-blooded aristocrats. Instead, they were common people.

They Are 'Rich in Faith'

Although the poor may lack earthly resources, James informs us that they are "rich in faith" (James 2:5). The word "rich" here is the Greek word *plousios*, and it describes *wealth so great it cannot be tabulated*. It is *vast wealth*, *extreme riches, and incredible abundance*. Interestingly, it is the very word used by Plato to say no one was richer than legendary King Midas.

The Holy Spirit prompted the apostle Paul to use this word *plousios* in Ephesians 2:4 when he informed us of how "rich" in mercy God is. The use of this word here is the equivalent of saying, "When it comes to mercy, God has so much it cannot be tabulated!" We could even say that He is *filthy, stinking, rich* when it comes to mercy, which is wonderful because we desperately need it! His mercy is continually flowing to us anew every day, and the supply is never-ending!

Even if you came to Christ when you were dirt poor and destitute, that is not your destiny. The Bible declares that one of the primary reasons Jesus came was to "preach the gospel to the poor" (Luke 4:18). This lets us know that the preaching of the Gospel is an economic game-changer. It has supernatural ability to reverse the curse of poverty and drastically upgrade our economic status.

In the context of James 2:5, the use of the word "rich" (*plousios*) indicates that God has purposely chosen the poor and destitute by the world's standards to be *filthy, stinking rich in faith*. Friend, it is His intent to give you so much faith it cannot be measured! And if you're rich in faith, everything else in your life will change for the better. It's only a matter of time. Just think about the many kinds of riches faith in Christ provides:

- We are rich in the fellowship and fullness of the Holy Spirit.
- We are rich in the gifts and fruit of the Holy Spirit.
- We are rich in the fellowship and camaraderie with other believers.
- We are rich in God's love, mercy, and grace.

Again, James said that God has "…chosen the poor of this world [to be] rich **in faith**…" (James 2:5). The words "in faith" — the Greek words *en pistei* — describes *a force that is moving forward*. Faith is like a bullet shot out of a gun, and when you release your faith, it's going to take you from where you are to a totally new place. Faith never leaves you in the same place. Because God has made you exceedingly rich in faith, your circumstances are in the process of improving.

We Are Coheirs With Christ

In addition to being made rich in faith, James said God transforms the poor into "heirs of the kingdom" (James 2:5). The word "heirs" here is the Greek word *kleronomos*, which describes *someone who inherits*. In ancient times, this word was used to depict *an inheritance*, *a title-deed*, *a legacy*, or *a heritable estate*.

For all who are in Christ, the lot has been cast in our favor, and we are *co-heirs* with Jesus (*see* Romans 8:17). That means everything that belongs to Christ also belongs to us. Wow! Our faith in Him and His promises becomes a dynamic force that is always moving us forward into the new things He has prepared for us — including our inheritance.

James says that our inheritance is the "kingdom." This word is a translation of the Greek word *basileia*, which describes *a realm of rule*. God's intention is for every person — regardless of their economic status — to eventually come to a place where they live life with reigning power. The Bible says this has been "...promised to them that love him" (James 2:5).

The word "promised" here is the Greek word *epangellomai*, and it describes *a promise*, *a guarantee*, or *a pledge* from God Himself. Being coheirs of the kingdom with Christ is God's personal promise and guarantee to everyone who loves Him and has placed their faith in Him.

Despising or Dishonoring the Poor Breaks God's Heart

When we come to James 2:6, we discover what the Jewish believers were doing in their churches. James wrote, "But ye have despised the poor...." The word "despised" here is the Greek word *atimadzo*, which is from the Greek word *time*, translated as "honor," but here it means *to dishonor or to insult*. It describes *shameful behavior toward another person*. Again, the word "poor" here is the Greek word *ptochos* and denotes *one who crouches or cowers like a beggar because he's embarrassed by his beggarly condition*. He is *deeply destitute and lacking in earthly resources.* This word *ptochos* is the very word for a *pauper.*

We already saw in the first four verses that when the poor came into the church services of these Jewish believers, the church leaders were telling them to stand off to the side or sit out of the sight of others. In contrast, the wealthy were given preferred seating and the red-carpet treatment. This discrimination regarding economic status was grievous in God's sight, and James let them know it.

Think about it. Very few people are born wealthy. Consequently, nearly every rich person had to start from the bottom and work their way up. The great news is that it doesn't matter what status you were born into. If you will grab hold of the Word of God and patiently continue to release the faith He gives you, that faith will grow and take you forward into your inheritance.

The 'Rich' Were Known for Harassing Christians and Blaspheming Jesus' Name

In his next breath, James asked his readers this question: "…Do not rich men oppress you, and draw you before the judgment seats?" (James 2:6) Here, he clearly reminded them that it was the rich — those they were giving preferred treatment to when they came to church — that were the ones harassing them. Specifically, James said, "…[They] draw you before the judgment seats" (James 2:6).

The word "draw" in Greek is *helkuo*, which means *to drag, lure,* or *draw, as into a snare.* And the word "before" is the Greek word *eis,* which means *into,* or *right into.* The rich were luring believers right into the "judgment seats," which in Greek describes *the courts — the place of arbitration; a place where judgment is given.* It was the rich who were suing the poor.

But that wasn't all. James continued his reality check by saying, "Do not they blaspheme that worthy name by the which ye are called?" (James 2:7) The word "blaspheme" here is *blasphemeo,* and it means *to slander, to accuse,* or *to speak against.* It denotes *derogatory words for the purpose of injuring or harming one's reputation,* and it also signifies *profane, foul, unclean language.* Moreover, this word can refer to *blaspheming the divine,* but in general, it is *any derogatory speech intended to defame, injure, or harm another's reputation.*

In a broader sense, it includes *nasty, shameful, ugly speech, or behavior intended to humiliate someone.*

Who were the rich blaspheming and purposely trying to injure with their words? James said, "...that worthy name by the which ye are called" (James 2:7). In Greek, the word "worthy" is *kalos,* and it describes *something good, noble, superior,* or *exceptional* — *something outstanding* or *of the highest quality.* And the word "name" is the Greek term *onoma,* which means *name* or *reputation.* James was directly referring to *the name of Jesus.* That is why he included the phrase "ye are called," which means *a name conferred upon you.*

When We Love Others Like God Loves Us, We Display Outstanding, Exceptional Behavior

When we come to James 2:8, James adds, "If ye fulfil the royal law according to the scripture, Thou shalt love thy neighbour as thyself, ye do well." The word "fulfill" here is *teleo* in Greek, and it means *to bring to fulfillment; to bring to maturity,* or *to complete.* In this case, he was referring to fulfilling and completing "the royal law" — "...Thou shalt *love* thy neighbor as thyself..." (James 2:8).

The word "love" here is a form of the Greek word *agape,* which describes *the love of God* — *the highest kind of love there is.* This *high-level love* is given to us unconditionally and has no strings attached. Jesus said we are to give this same love to our "neighbor," which is the Greek word *plesion,* and describes *the one nearby you; any person near you in some way.*

Just as the Jewish believers in the First Century were surrounded by all kinds of people, so are we. And what James told them he is also telling us. It doesn't matter what a person's economic status is, we're to love them with God's *agape,* high-level love. If we carry out this command, Scripture says we do "well." This word "well" is actually the same Greek word translated as "worthy" in verse 7. It is the word *kalos,* which depicts that which is *noble* or *good.* It refers to *superior behavior* or *something that is exceptional* and *of the highest quality.*

Friend, we are to love everyone with the unconditional love of God regardless of whether they're wealthy or dirt poor. Instead of judging people by their exterior appearance or by what they own or don't own, we need to ask God for His grace to treat everyone the way He treats us. Remember, the Gospel is an economic game changer. The poor who become believers won't always be poor. As they learn how to release their faith and become heirs of the Kingdom, they will experience the reality of God's promises and begin reigning in life with the rest of God's people.

STUDY QUESTIONS

Study to shew thyself approved unto God, a workman that needeth not to be ashamed, rightly dividing the word of truth.
— 2 Timothy 2:15

1. Which character quality of God is shown over and over again in Acts 10:34,35; Romans 2:11; Galatians 2:6; Ephesians 6:9; and Job 34:18,19? What does the fact that it appears so often in Scripture tell you about Him?

2. Has giving to the poor always been important to God? Does He actively help the poor Himself? And is there any benefit for us when we follow Him in this area? Read the following verses to find out: Deuteronomy 15:7,11; First Samuel 2:8; Psalm 40:17; 41:1; Proverbs 14:31; 19:17; Isaiah 41:17; Second Corinthians 8:9; and James 2:14-17.

3. What does it mean to be "rich in faith"? What can riches like that enable us to do? Check out Hebrews 11 for some practical examples.

PRACTICAL APPLICATION

But be ye doers of the word, and not hearers only, deceiving your own selves.
— James 1:22

It can be easier than we might think to subconsciously favor (or be offended with) someone based on their socioeconomic status, especially in church. That's why it's so important to pay attention to how we're treating people. Take a moment to think through these questions and answer them honestly, even if only to yourself.

1. When was the last time you interacted with someone you perceived as wealthy? How much time and attention did you give them? What assumptions did you have about them/their situation?

2. Now think back to a time when you talked with someone you perceived as broke or poor. How much of your time and attention did they receive? What did you assume about them/their situation based on your conversation?

3. After going through this lesson, what do you think you should do differently going forward?

As you already know, it's incredibly important to God that we don't show favoritism. Whatever your answers were, ask the Holy Spirit for the grace to see, love and treat every person the way *He* does.

4. Can you think of any person or group (i.e. a ministry, political party, social group, family member, etc.) that you've been offended with because they seem to have massive amounts of money? Once they come to mind, ask God to forgive you for holding onto offense and pray for them (*see* 1 Peter 3:8,9). (*Remember that money never ultimately equates joy, health, closeness with God, success, impact or relationships, so even someone with a lot of money may be genuinely miserable while appearing happy and fulfilled.)

Notes

Notes

Notes

www.ingramcontent.com/pod-product-compliance
Lightning Source LLC
Chambersburg PA
CBHW051047030426
42339CB00006B/229